Words can lift you up...
and they can bring you down

So choose to be a lyrical boss
who's goodness is renowned!

- Make it Happen Publishing

Send all inquires to: books@mihpublishing.com

Make it Happen Publishing Inc.

RAPPER*notes*

Make it Happen Publishing Inc.

How to Write a Rap Song
Basic Tips and Structure of a Rap Song

STEP 1: Brainstorm ideas, themes, inspirations, metaphors, stories
- *this is where you should come up with some hook/chorus ideas*
- *choose topics you are passionate about and that you know*
- *jot down key words that describe your topic*
- *make a list of words that rhyme with your main key words (rhyme clusters)*
- *avoid using words just because they rhyme*
- *remember not all your lines have to rhyme*
- *tell a full story (make sure your rap has a beginning, middle and end)*
- *look to your poems and your favorite rap artists for inspiration*

STEP 2: Choose a couple of beats to experiment with for feel and speed
- *find free beats online, from existing soundtracks or create your own*
- *metronomes help to keep track of the beat*
- *raps normally have 4 beats per bar/line but you can go faster or slower*
- *raps normally have 8 bars/lines per chorus/hook*
- *raps normally have 16 bars/lines per verse*

STEP 3: Write some lyrics and match them to your beat
- *the syllables in each line will be the basis of your beat*
- *divide your words into syllables to make it easier to match your beat*
- *the more words you add to a line, the faster the beat will be*
- *create some rhyming schemes for your verses (how the rap will rhyme)*
- *set up a rap structure for your rap (you can really do what you want)*

   Some examples:
   1. Verse-Chorus-Verse-Chorus-Verse-Chorus (Intro & Outro omitted)
   2. Intro-Chorus-Verse-Chorus-Verse-Chorus-Outro
   3. Intro-Verse-Chorus-Verse-Chorus-Verse-Chorus-Outro
   4. Intro-Hook-Verse-Hook-Bridge-Verse-Chorus-Outro

STEP 4: Practice your rap over and over and make edits if it's needed
- *when practicing, listen for what is working or not working*
- *make any changes to help the flow of your lyrics*
- *add emotion to your rap so people can feel it through your words*
- *practice projecting your voice while you rap*

STEP 5: Now perform it, record it and share it with the world!
- *this is your masterpiece - so take pride in it but also be open to critique, comments and suggestions from your audience*
- *the only way to get better at writing and performing your raps is so keep writing and performing*
- *the most important thing is to enjoy the process!*

Common Rap Structure
Experiment and be creative with your own RAP structure!

INTRO

	Beat 1	Beat 2	Beat 3	Beat 4	
Bar 1					**Normally 4 Beats per Bar/Line and up to 8 Bars**
Bar 2					(not always included)
Bar 3					
Bar 4					
Bar 5					*Can be speech, sound effects or other noises*
Bar 6					
Bar 7					**1 Bar = 1 Line of Rap**
Bar 8					**4 Bars = 1 Quatrain**

CHORUS/HOOK

Bar 1					**Usually repeated 3 to 4 times during the rap song**
Bar 2					
Bar 3					Normally it's 1 quatrain repeated twice to make 8 bars total
Bar 4					
Bar 5					
Bar 6					*This is where the main idea and meaning of your rap is described to peek the audience's attention*
Bar 7					
Bar 8					

VERSE

Bar 1					
Bar 2					
Bar 3					
Bar 4					**Usually repeated 3 times during the rap song**
Bar 5					
Bar 6					
Bar 7					**16 Bars per Verse**
Bar 8					Can be 8, 12, 16 or 24 bars - most raps have 16 bars
Bar 9					
Bar 10					*This is where you rap about the topic - make the points to support your overall theme*
Bar 11					
Bar 12					
Bar 13					
Bar 14					
Bar 15					
Bar 16					

CHORUS >>VERSE>>CHORUS>>VERSE>>CHORUS
Repeat the chorus and verse as many times as you like

AFTER/BEFORE CHORUS and/or BRIDGE
- Not necessary but you can add a few lines of rap before or after your chorus to assist it or a bridge between two choruses (add the bridge near the end of the rap to add more interest to the lyrics)

OUTRO

Bar 1					
Bar 2					
Bar 3					**Up to 8 Bars** (not always included)
Bar 4					
Bar 5					*Can be anything to lower the energy level and end off the rap*
Bar 6					
Bar 7					
Bar 8					

Rhyme Scheme Patterns
Here are a few different ways to make your RAP rhyme

TYPE OF RHYMES:

End Rhymes – The last word of the line rhymes.
Internal Rhymes – Two words in the same line rhymes.
Slant or Near Rhymes – The vowel or consonant sounds of two words in the same line rhymes (the sound of the words are similar but do not actually rhyme).
Identical Rhymes – When the same word is used again.

X = Line does not RHYME   *) = Lines RHYME*

Most Common Words Used in RAP
Add to the list with your own personal favorite words

SUGGESTIONS:

These are a few of the most common words found in popular rap culture - that does not mean you must stick to this list. Use it as a point of reference but you should absolutely be original and write rap that is inspired by your own ideas, thoughts and experiences.

Balling	Mane	_____
Beef	Money	_____
Benz	Nike	_____
Biggie	Nina	_____
Block	Pimping	_____
Blunts	Popping	_____
Bro	Project	_____
Cash	Rack	_____
Chopper	Rapper	_____
Claim	Realest	_____
Clique	Rep	_____
Coupe	Sayin	_____
Crew	Shooter	_____
Def	Slug	_____
Deuce	Snitch	_____
Dope	Squad	_____
Flex	Stack	_____
Flexing	Stacking	_____
Fresh	Stash	_____
Gangsta	Strapped	_____
Gat	Struggle	_____
Gonna	Stunting	_____
Goon	Swang	_____
Groupie	Tech	_____
Holla	Trapping	_____
Homeboy	Trill	_____
Homey	Westside	_____
Hood	Wit	_____
Hustle	Yo	_____
Mac	Yup	_____

* Profanity words and words that may be considered offensive have been omitted from this list
* Add to this list with your own favorite rap words

Common Slang Words

Here's a list of common slang terms used in RAP

24/7 = all day hustle
100 = truthful
411 = information
730 = insane or unstable
Bag of Sand/Hand Bag/Sheckles = money
Baller = a high-roller, money maker
Beef = conflict
Bounce/Dip/Jet = to leave/go
Brass = funny
Brick = $200,000
Chill/Chillin'/Chillax = relax/relaxing, keep cool
Da Bomb = cool, appealing or popular
Dancing with the Devil = doing something risky
Dime = a good looking female
Dukes = parents
Flex = show off
Fly = cool
Front = pretending to be what you are not
Getty = a get together with friends
Grub = food
Handful = $5
Heated = very angry
K/Stack = $1000
Mill = 1 million dollars
Off the Chain = unbelievable
OG = original gangster
Old Man = father
Pad/Crib = home
Peace Out = goodbye
Po-Po/Popes = police/feds/cops
Pots of Money = to have lots of cash
Fo'shizzle = for sure
Scrilla/Scrappa/Dibs/Measures = cash
Shook = scared
Tick = heart or heart beating
Ton/Benji/C-Note = $100
Wack = crazy, stupid or to kill
Whip = car
Word Up = you got that right
Yard = your house

Resources to find Words that Rhyme
Useful websites to find the right words for your RAP

Rhyming & Helpful Rap Websites:

www.b-rhymes.com
www.colemizestudios.com
www.dillfrog.com
www.double-rhyme.com
www.genius.com
www.rapmetrics.com
www.rappad.co
www.rapscript.net
www.rhymebrain.com
www.rhymebuster.com
www.rhymer.com
www.rhymezone.com

Other Rap Resource:

www.audiosauna.com
www.deepbeat.org
www.handmetheaux.com
www.hiphopdx.com
www.lyricsfreak.com
www.metronomer.com
www.musicindustryhowto.com
www.myrapname.com
www.rapanalysis.com
www.rapbasement.com
www.rappingmanual.com
www.reverbnation.com
www.smartrapper.com
www.song-lyrics-generator.org.uk
www.wikihow.com/Rap
www.writeexpress.com
www.writerbot.com

My Favorite Rap Resources:

1 _____
2 _____
3 _____
4 _____
5 _____
6 _____
7 _____
8 _____
9 _____
10 _____
11 _____
12 _____
13 _____
14 _____
15 _____
16 _____
17 _____
18 _____
19 _____
20 _____
21 _____
22 _____
23 _____
24 _____
25 _____

My Favorite Rappers, Raps & Lyrics

Keep track of those who inspire you!

Rap Brainstorming Notes

Jot down any ideas or rhymes that might work in your RAP

RAP TITLE: _____

Date: _____

INTRO

CHORUS/HOOK

VERSE

OUTRO

NOTES

Rap Brainstorming Notes

Jot down any ideas or rhymes that might work in your RAP

RAP TITLE: _____

Date: _____

INTRO

CHORUS/HOOK

VERSE

OUTRO

NOTES

Rap Brainstorming Notes

Jot down any ideas or rhymes that might work in your RAP

RAP TITLE: _____

Date: _____

INTRO

CHORUS/HOOK

VERSE

OUTRO

NOTES

Rap Brainstorming Notes
Jot down any ideas or rhymes that might work in your RAP

RAP TITLE: _____

Date: _____

INTRO

CHORUS/HOOK

VERSE

OUTRO

NOTES

Rap Brainstorming Notes

Jot down any ideas or rhymes that might work in your RAP

RAP TITLE: _____

Date: _____

INTRO

CHORUS/HOOK

VERSE

OUTRO

NOTES

Rap Brainstorming Notes

Jot down any ideas or rhymes that might work in your RAP

RAP TITLE: _____

Date: _____

INTRO

CHORUS/HOOK

VERSE

OUTRO

NOTES

Rap Brainstorming Notes

Jot down any ideas or rhymes that might work in your RAP

RAP TITLE: _____

Date: _____

INTRO

CHORUS/HOOK

VERSE

OUTRO

NOTES

Rap Brainstorming Notes

Jot down any ideas or rhymes that might work in your RAP

RAP TITLE: _____

Date: _____

INTRO

CHORUS/HOOK

VERSE

OUTRO

NOTES

Rap Brainstorming Notes

Jot down any ideas or rhymes that might work in your RAP

RAP TITLE: _____

Date: _____

INTRO

CHORUS/HOOK

VERSE

OUTRO

NOTES

Rap Brainstorming Notes

Jot down any ideas or rhymes that might work in your RAP

RAP TITLE: _____

Date: _____

INTRO

CHORUS/HOOK

VERSE

OUTRO

NOTES

Rap Brainstorming Notes

Jot down any ideas or rhymes that might work in your RAP

RAP TITLE: _____

Date: _____

INTRO

CHORUS/HOOK

VERSE

OUTRO

NOTES

Rap Brainstorming Notes

Jot down any ideas or rhymes that might work in your RAP

RAP TITLE: _____

Date: _____

INTRO

CHORUS/HOOK

VERSE

OUTRO

NOTES

Rap Brainstorming Notes

Jot down any ideas or rhymes that might work in your RAP

RAP TITLE: _____

Date: _____

INTRO

CHORUS/HOOK

VERSE

OUTRO

NOTES

Rap Brainstorming Notes

Jot down any ideas or rhymes that might work in your RAP

RAP TITLE: _____

Date: _____

INTRO

CHORUS/HOOK

VERSE

OUTRO

NOTES

Rap Brainstorming Notes

Jot down any ideas or rhymes that might work in your RAP

RAP TITLE: _____

Date: _____

INTRO

CHORUS/HOOK

VERSE

OUTRO

NOTES

Rap Brainstorming Notes

Jot down any ideas or rhymes that might work in your RAP

RAP TITLE: _____

Date: _____

INTRO

CHORUS/HOOK

VERSE

OUTRO

NOTES

Rap Brainstorming Notes

Jot down any ideas or rhymes that might work in your RAP

RAP TITLE: _____

Date: _____

INTRO

CHORUS/HOOK

VERSE

OUTRO

NOTES

Rap Brainstorming Notes

Jot down any ideas or rhymes that might work in your RAP

RAP TITLE: _____

Date: _____

INTRO

CHORUS/HOOK

VERSE

OUTRO

NOTES

Rap Brainstorming Notes

Jot down any ideas or rhymes that might work in your RAP

RAP TITLE: _____

Date: _____

INTRO

CHORUS/HOOK

VERSE

OUTRO

NOTES

Rap Brainstorming Notes

Jot down any ideas or rhymes that might work in your RAP

RAP TITLE: _____

Date: _____

INTRO

CHORUS/HOOK

VERSE

OUTRO

NOTES

Rap Brainstorming Notes

Jot down any ideas or rhymes that might work in your RAP

RAP TITLE: _____

Date: _____

INTRO

CHORUS/HOOK

VERSE

OUTRO

NOTES

Rap Brainstorming Notes

Jot down any ideas or rhymes that might work in your RAP

RAP TITLE: _____

Date: _____

INTRO

CHORUS/HOOK

VERSE

OUTRO

NOTES

Rap Brainstorming Notes

Jot down any ideas or rhymes that might work in your RAP

INTRO

CHORUS/HOOK

VERSE

OUTRO

NOTES

Rap Brainstorming Notes

Jot down any ideas or rhymes that might work in your RAP

RAP TITLE: _____

Date: _____

Rap Brainstorming Notes

Jot down any ideas or rhymes that might work in your RAP

RAP TITLE: _____

Date: _____

INTRO

CHORUS/HOOK

VERSE

OUTRO

NOTES

Rap Brainstorming Notes

Jot down any ideas or rhymes that might work in your RAP

RAP TITLE: _____

Date: _____

INTRO

CHORUS/HOOK

VERSE

OUTRO

NOTES

Rap Brainstorming Notes

Jot down any ideas or rhymes that might work in your RAP

RAP TITLE: _____

Date: _____

INTRO

CHORUS/HOOK

VERSE

OUTRO

NOTES

Rap Brainstorming Notes

Jot down any ideas or rhymes that might work in your RAP

RAP TITLE: _____

Date: _____

INTRO

CHORUS/HOOK

VERSE

OUTRO

NOTES

Rap Brainstorming Notes

Jot down any ideas or rhymes that might work in your RAP

RAP TITLE: _____

Date: _____

INTRO

CHORUS/HOOK

VERSE

OUTRO

NOTES

Rap Brainstorming Notes

Jot down any ideas or rhymes that might work in your RAP

RAP TITLE: _____

Date: _____

INTRO

CHORUS/HOOK

VERSE

OUTRO

NOTES

Rap Brainstorming Notes

Jot down any ideas or rhymes that might work in your RAP

RAP TITLE: _____

Date: _____

INTRO

CHORUS/HOOK

VERSE

OUTRO

NOTES

Rap Brainstorming Notes

Jot down any ideas or rhymes that might work in your RAP

RAP TITLE: _____

Date: _____

INTRO

CHORUS/HOOK

VERSE

OUTRO

NOTES

Rap Brainstorming Notes

Jot down any ideas or rhymes that might work in your RAP

RAP TITLE: _____

Date: _____

INTRO

CHORUS/HOOK

VERSE

OUTRO

NOTES

Rap Brainstorming Notes

Jot down any ideas or rhymes that might work in your RAP

RAP TITLE: _____

Date: _____

INTRO

CHORUS/HOOK

VERSE

OUTRO

NOTES

Rap Brainstorming Notes

Jot down any ideas or rhymes that might work in your RAP

INTRO

CHORUS/HOOK

VERSE

OUTRO

NOTES

Rap Brainstorming Notes

Jot down any ideas or rhymes that might work in your RAP

RAP TITLE: _____

Date: _____

INTRO

CHORUS/HOOK

VERSE

OUTRO

NOTES

Rap Brainstorming Notes

Jot down any ideas or rhymes that might work in your RAP

RAP TITLE: _____

Date: _____

INTRO

CHORUS/HOOK

VERSE

OUTRO

NOTES

Rap Brainstorming Notes

Jot down any ideas or rhymes that might work in your RAP

RAP TITLE: _____

Date: _____

INTRO

CHORUS/HOOK

VERSE

OUTRO

NOTES

Rap Brainstorming Notes

Jot down any ideas or rhymes that might work in your RAP

RAP TITLE: _____

Date: _____

INTRO

CHORUS/HOOK

VERSE

OUTRO

NOTES

Rap Brainstorming Notes

Jot down any ideas or rhymes that might work in your RAP

RAP TITLE: _____

Date: _____

INTRO

CHORUS/HOOK

VERSE

OUTRO

NOTES

Rap Brainstorming Notes

Jot down any ideas or rhymes that might work in your RAP

RAP TITLE: _____

Date: _____

INTRO

CHORUS/HOOK

VERSE

OUTRO

NOTES

Rap Brainstorming Notes

Jot down any ideas or rhymes that might work in your RAP

RAP TITLE: _____

Date: _____

INTRO

CHORUS/HOOK

VERSE

OUTRO

NOTES

Rap Brainstorming Notes
Jot down any ideas or rhymes that might work in your RAP

RAP TITLE: _____

Date: _____

INTRO

CHORUS/HOOK

VERSE

OUTRO

NOTES

Rap Brainstorming Notes

Jot down any ideas or rhymes that might work in your RAP

INTRO

CHORUS/HOOK

VERSE

OUTRO

NOTES

Rap Brainstorming Notes

Jot down any ideas or rhymes that might work in your RAP

RAP TITLE: _____

Date: _____

INTRO

CHORUS/HOOK

VERSE

OUTRO

NOTES

Made in the USA
Las Vegas, NV
13 October 2021